Connecticut

By Susan Evento

Consultant
Donna Loughran
Reading Consultant

Children's Press®
A Division of Scholastic Inc.
New York   Toronto   London   Auckland   Sydney
Mexico City   New Delhi   Hong Kong
Danbury, Connecticut

Designer: Herman Adler Design
Photo Researcher: Caroline Anderson
The photo on the cover shows a Connecticut dairy farm during autumn.

Library of Congress Cataloging-in-Publication Data

Evento, Susan.
  Connecticut / by Susan Evento ; consultant, Donna Loughran.
    p. cm. — (Rookie read-about geography)
    Includes index.
    ISBN 0-516-22751-3 (lib. bdg.)   0-516-25927-X (pbk.)
    1. Connecticut—Juvenile literature. 2. Connecticut—Geography—Juvenile
  literature. I. Vargus, Nanci Reginelli. II. Title. III. Series.
    F94.3.E95 2004
    974.6'044—dc22
                                    2004000467

CHILDREN'S PRESS, and ROOKIE READ-ABOUT®,
and associated logos are trademarks and or registered trademarks
of Scholastic Library Publishing. SCHOLASTIC and associated logos
are trademarks and or registered trademarks of Scholastic Inc.

1 2 3 4 5 6 7 8 9 10 R 13 12 11 10 09 08 07 06 05 04

Which state gave us the first lollipop?

Connecticut did!

Can you find Connecticut on this map?

It is in the northeastern part of the United States.

CANADA

WASHINGTON

OREGON

IDAHO

MONTANA

NORTH DAKOTA

SOUTH DAKOTA

WYOMING

MINNESOTA

WISCONSIN

MICHIGAN

NEW HAMPSHIRE

VERMONT

MAINE

MASSACHUSETTS

RHODE ISLAND

CONNECTICUT

NEW YORK

PENNSYLVANIA

NEW JERSEY

DELAWARE

MARYLAND

Washington, D.C.

NEVADA

UTAH

COLORADO

NEBRASKA

IOWA

ILLINOIS

INDIANA

OHIO

WEST VIRGINIA

VIRGINIA

CALIFORNIA

KANSAS

MISSOURI

KENTUCKY

NORTH CAROLINA

ARIZONA

NEW MEXICO

OKLAHOMA

ARKANSAS

TENNESSEE

SOUTH CAROLINA

ALABAMA

GEORGIA

TEXAS

MISSISSIPPI

LOUISIANA

FLORIDA

North

West   East

South

ALASKA   CANADA

MEXICO

HAWAII

5

Hartford

Connecticut is the
third-smallest state in
the United States.

More than 3 million
people live in Connecticut.
Hartford is the state capital.

Connecticut has many rivers and streams.

The Connecticut River is the main river. It almost cuts the state in half.

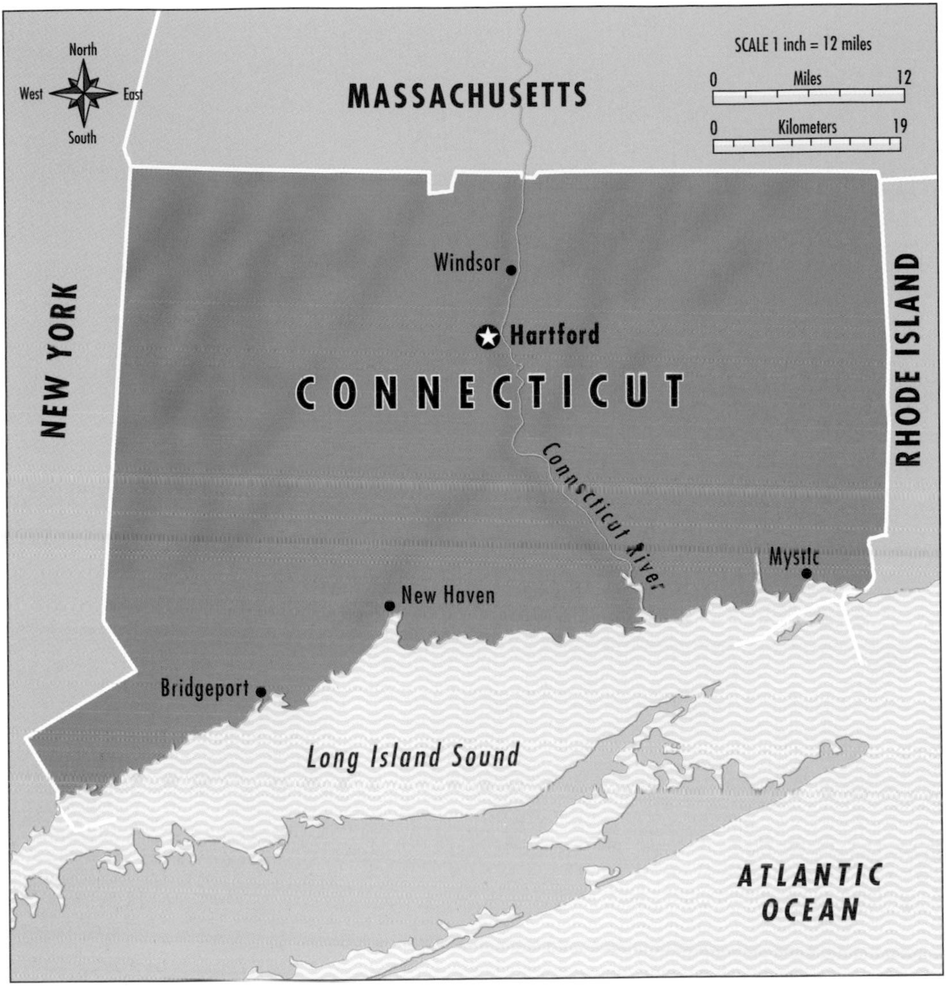
North
West
East
South
MASSACHUSETTS
SCALE 1 inch = 12 miles
0
Miles
12
0
Kilometers
19
NEW YORK
RHODE ISLAND
Windsor
Hartford
CONNECTICUT
Connecticut River
Mystic
New Haven
Bridgeport
Long Island Sound
ATLANTIC
OCEAN

Connecticut River

The land around the
Connecticut River is flat.

There are low mountains
in the western part of
Connecticut. There are
hills in the east.

Connecticut has many forests. There are hickory, maple, oak, and pine trees in these forests.

Robin

Orioles and robins live
in the forests. The robin
is the state bird.

Connecticut has more than 1,000 lakes. Muskrats, otters, and minks live near the water.

Otters

Mystic Seaport

There are many things
to do in Connecticut.

You can visit Mystic
Seaport. It has a village
that looks very old.

It has old wooden ships
you can climb aboard, too.

First, Native Americans from the Algonquin (al-GONG-kwin) tribes lived in Connecticut.

Then, Dutch explorers came. English settlers came, too. They built the first Connecticut town. It was called Windsor.

Algonquins

A factory

Many things were started in Connecticut.

The first town library started here. So did the first newspaper.

Connecticut had the first factory town, too.

Factories in Connecticut make jet engines, helicopters, and submarines.

They make machines, computers, and plastics, too.

Jet engine factory

Yale University

Schools are important in
Connecticut.

Yale University is the
third-oldest college in
the United States.

Many people visit Connecticut every year.

They go to see dogwood trees bloom in the spring. They go to see leaves change color in the fall.

Dogwood trees

28

They play on the beach
in the summer, too.

Would you like to visit
Connecticut one day?

Words You Know

Connecticut River

dogwood trees

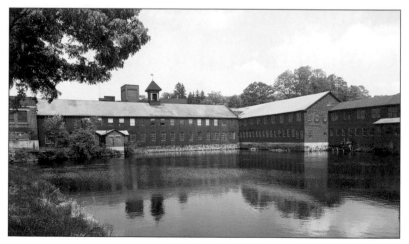

factory

Mystic Seaport

otters

robin

Yale University

31

Index

About the Author

Susan Evento is a former teacher. For the past 16 years she has been a writer and editor of books and instructional materials. Recently, she was the Editorial Director of *Creative Classroom* magazine, an award-winning K–8 national teacher's magazine. Evento lives in New York city with her partner and three cats.

Photo Credits

Photographs © 2004: Corbis Images/Robin Prange: cover; Corbis Sygma: 3; McConnell & McNamara/Jack McConell: 6, 10, 12, 16, 20, 23, 30 top left, 30 bottom, 31 top left; Minden Pictures/Gerry Ellis: 15, 31 top right; North Wind Picture Archives: 19; Superstock, Inc./Joseph Barnell: 27, 30 top right; The Image Works/Peter Hvizdak: 24, 28, 31 bottom right; Visuals Unlimited/Barbara Gerlach: 13, 31 bottom left.

Maps by Bob Italiano